5

GW00992351

то

GET HELP
from
GOD

Vernon Howard

Copyright 1981
NEW LIFE FOUNDATION
4th Printing
ISBN 0-911203-11-7

50 WAYS TO GET HELP FROM GOD

Have you lost confidence in help from other people? Can you no longer believe in your usual hopes? Are you unable to trust what you used to rely upon?

Excellent! Marvelous!

Congratulations!

You are just the person for whom this publication is intended.

Far above human weakness is God, Truth, Reality. In this publication we will use these three terms to describe the Spiritual Power which will rescue any man or woman who truly wishes rescue.

You can solve all problems, no matter how long they have tormented you. You can clear away all painful conditions, regardless of how strongly stubborn they seem to be.

It just so happens that God is not bothered by anything. After making contact with God, you won't be bothered either. There will be no one to be bothered. There will just be your Understanding. And Understanding is peace.

There are no exceptions to the kind of unwanted conditions you can toss out. You will overwhelm everything that now overwhelms you. Here are just a few of the burdens that will fall away: fear of making wrong decisions, aching loneliness, worry over losing someone, daily stress, shame over past mistakes, dark depression, anger toward people who used you and left you, chronic anxiety, feeling surrounded by threats. Just as the rising sun conquers *all* darkness, so does the light of Truth make all your difficulties disappear.

A story was once written about a man who found a Great Secret. It told of a former business executive who searched for and discovered an entirely new kind of civilization of peaceful people and pleasant days. With these powerful teachings you can also be someone with a Great Secret. Your new world will be inner and everlasting.

There is a strange reason why people

fail to get help from God. It is extremely important for you to know this reason. Insight into it is a strong contribution toward your success as a human being.

People fail to contact God because they refuse to see that the human condition is far worse than it appears to be on the surface. Follow this reasoning carefully.

People fear to face the full horror of the human situation because by doing so they would have to admit that they have neither a personal nor national solution. They deceive themselves with the assurance, "Well, since there is no serious problem we need not go chasing around for a drastic solution. See how practical we are?" Their foolish minds are now convinced that a cure is pointless because the sickness is absent. This is the worst kind of destructive self-deception. *They fear to face the fact that they don't know the answers*. And so they sit back and let their unseen lunacy rule and ruin themselves and everyone else. And if an evil ever becomes too obvious to avoid it is, of course, always the other person's wickedness.

And God is left completely out of it. You can see why Truth and Reality can have no place in their schemes. A self-worshipper cannot tolerate anything that threatens to expose his beloved delusions. His answers to threats are hateful attacks.

On rare occasions in human history a unique individual comes along. He is truly a heaven-sent teacher with a message for all who want to listen. He says something like this: "Listen! I have good news for you. You have every reason to be cheerful and confident. You can solve the mystery of life. But first you must admit that your days are painful puzzles to you. So face the wreckage that surrounds you while knowing fully that you don't have the answers. Don't fear that fact and don't be ashamed of it. Your shame indicates your vanity's belief that *it* must create the solution, which is all wrong. You need only have the courage to remain without *your* answer, for that humility is what attracts the real answer to you. See the storm of your life. Enter it without asking what will happen to you. Pass thru the storm, for on the other side is everything for which your heart deeply yearns. Come, I will personally guide you thru the storm until you reach the safety of the other side."

Ponder the pleasant necessity for finding your real nature. It exists beneath all the artificialities imposed on you by both a ruthless society and your own unawareness of what was going on. You must discover who you really are because only your real self can make contact with rescuing Reality. The false self can *do* nothing for it *is* nothing. The false self is unusable, but foolish men and women still try to employ it. Nothing is sadder or more frustrating than for a man to try to climb to heaven on the ladder of self-delusion. And the more you try to show him what he is doing against himself the hotter flares his anger, for he thinks you are ridiculing him.

All this means that a sincere seeker of God's help must have no such resistances to spiritual information. He must see that Truth's only motive is to help, not hurt. It is something else that causes all the pain--resistance itself.

It makes no difference if you do not understand these principles at first. That is the usual course for everyone. So just relax and enjoy the inner adventure. On your first several readings make it your aim to simply *absorb* the healthy impressions that come to you. Absorption comes first, then understanding, just as the earth absorbs the seed which then turns into a flower. The following story makes the point clear.

A schoolboy was given a history book to read. A few hours later he told the teacher, "I can't understand it." The teacher asked, "What do you do when you can't understand a new game out on the playground?"

"Oh, that's easy," replied the boy, "I just keep playing until I see what it's all about."

The boy then understood and appreciated

7

the teacher's gentle way of helping him.

Take that same lighthearted attitude toward these higher facts. Your interested attention guarantees learning.

Here are three exercises that will help you over the weeks and months as you read this publication.

1. Give special attention to the first sentences on each of the 50 ways. They are among the most powerful spiritual facts ever given to humanity. They can change everything you want to change. See for yourself how wise and strong and encouraging they are. See that their only concern is for your swift flight to higher levels of life. Memorize those that inspire your feelings in a special way.

2. Write down the numbers of the items that refer to a present problem you have. Perhaps you fear that someone may deceive and hurt you. Or maybe you don't know how to find real strength and confidence. Make a list of which of the 50 ways discuss your difficulty. Go over the listed items several times. See

that they are showing you the way out, which you need only follow. Your acceptance of what is true is the same as your acceptance of the solution to your problem.

3. Suppose a man wants to build a secure and comfortable home, so first he collects the necessary lumber. He next goes into action with that lumber and soon has what he wants. Likewise, go into personal and inner action with these principles. For example, notice that: a. You really are tired of being afraid of this deceitful world. b. Your relatives and friends spend their entire lives in strained pretense that everything is all right. c. You sense that true help must come from a source higher than your own present mind. This noticing is a unique kind of action that builds your secure and comfortable inner home.

There is God, and there is you. But there is a third necessity. Something must serve as a bridge to connect the human and the Spiritual. You will now read about 50 solid bridges by which you can cross over to the help you need.

The help is over there right now, waiting for your arrival. You can start crossing right now.

1. *All you need to know is that you want out.* Imagine a man exploring a vast cave who suddenly realizes he is lost. His very awareness of his hazardous situation makes him want to get out. Likewise, you need only realize that you are lost in life. Your honesty about your actual condition is a request for help that reaches God. Never mind *how* you will get out. You have done your part. You now easily follow God's guidance toward the light.

2. *Your first duty in life is toward your own spiritual health.* It is not toward another human being or human activity. You are not being selfish when you make inner wholeness your first choice in life. You are obeying God's law. When deeply realized this acts like a compass that guides you toward the help you wish. It is also great relief, for all your false responsibilities and painful guilts will fall away. Life is then truly exciting, for at last you are finding yourself!

10

3. *You don't have to put up with it anymore.* Not one day longer. What is it you can give up? Feeling victimized, a noisy mind, unpleasant people, nightmare conditions and all else bad. Success requires that you turn in the right direction, which is to build a spirit that wants to know what life is really all about. Don't turn toward grief or gloom. *You don't have to put up with it anymore so don't put up with it anymore.*

4. *Don't live at the mercy of other people.* Are you easily upset by angry words and sour looks? It hurts only because you don't know who you are as yet. One day you were someone who was accepted and liked, but the next day you are someone who is rejected. *You are not someone who can be made or broken by the opinions of others.* You are your spiritual nature, which is free from all mere ideas, including your own. You know who you are when you don't have to think about it.

5. *Be as helpless as you feel you are.* God can help only a spiritually helpless person. It's not shameful to admit you cannot help yourself—it is very wise. Don't fear that you will fall apart by letting go of yourself. There is nothing to fear. The exact opposite will finally happen—you will come together in self-wholeness. Being helpless means to switch your loyalty from the false strength of egotism to God. Now you will be helped!

6. You are more intelligent than your troubles. A king stood on his castle wall as the enemy approached below. When asked why he was unafraid the king said, "He is bluffing—trying to make me think he has a thousand soldiers." Never credit troubles with power. They have none. God rules over all. So you don't have to solve problems. You need only see thru them. When you shake over a problem ask, "Would this bother the king?" No, and it also can't bother your true and royal nature.

7. You are never alone in your search. You have thousands of workers ready to obey your command. They are called spiritual facts. You can have as many as you wish. What you can't

12

do, they can. And they will prove their power. Higher facts always succeed for you, just as the wind always succeeds in sailing the boat forward. *See them as eager workers, turn them loose to win for you.* You will sail beyond secret sorrow.

8. Understand right and wrong questions. As you seek help from God you will ask all sorts of questions. See the difference between beneficial and useless questions. Do not ask how long it will take or why it is so complicated. Inquire earnestly. Ask why you resist Truth. Ask the cause for your haunting feeling of emptiness. Ask why your mind wanders away so frequently. Ask how you can give up a self-harming attitude. Practical questions attract helpful replies.

9. Proceed with the self-discovery even when afraid to do so. You have just met a mighty power called Even When Afraid. If your inner search reveals more anger or pretense or foolishness than you thought you had, continue in spite of the frightful shock. When afraid of anything you see in yourself, be afraid, but march on. You are marching out of darkness! God accompanies anyone who proceeds Even When Afraid.

10. *You can know what to do with yourself.* Sadly, most people have no idea of what to do with their lives. Even when busy they are busy doing nothing. In their confusion they just invent wasteful activities. They end up right back where they started. Yield to Truth. It will give your life meaning and purpose. You will find the enormous and constant pleasure of finding inner riches. You will rise above both yourself and the world. It's nice up there!

11. *Let a quiet mind be ready to receive.* Imagine a man who goes to a library and asks for a certain book. The librarian tries to supply the information, but the man never stops talking. He says how badly he wants the book, explains his long search for it, and on and on. People fail to find the rescuing facts because they prefer *mental chattering* to *spiritual receiving*. Want days without emotional stress and without mental warfare? Go silent.

12. Win the pleasure of right feelings. Want to feel good? It is really quite easy. You will feel emotional pleasure when: a. You understand there can be no happiness in fighting for happiness. b. You see that personal strength must come from personal rightness. c. You know that cheerfulness comes as wrongness goes. d. You realize that society's ways are trivial. e. You sense a fresh and pure spirit coming from a new source. f. You feel that now is the time to climb to a higher life.

13. Practice at interrupting mechanical thoughts. This classic spiritual exercise works wonders for you. Interrupt your usual thoughts by becoming conscious of whatever you are doing at the moment. Don't get lost in thought, but be aware of yourself breathing, talking, lifting a cup, nodding your head. Turn your attention back on yourself and catch yourself in action. In these moments you are *seeing,* not *thinking,* which makes life a pleasure.

14. Ask God to give you guiding light. That

request is always honored. At once. God will supply as much light as you can take. Light solves all problems. If you don't like stumbling over your furniture in a dark room, just turn on the light. If you don't like bumping into life and getting hurt, just request spiritual light. The hurts will go. Do you ask, "What can I do about my problems?" You have just been given an extremely practical answer. Go into action with it.

15. Don't allow suffering to have its way. Most people meekly submit to mental pain because it seems to be so persistently powerful. Nonsense. Agony is nothing but a bluff and a fake and a liar. Call its bluff and it will sneak away like the cruel coward that it is. But don't fight it, for that only increases its energy. Instead, right in the middle of the pain, practice self-release. Let go of all your usual efforts to chase away pain. Truth will do the rest.

16. Notice how everyone resists helpful truths. People fear that Truth will take something valuable from them, when all it takes are their pains. Don't fear a fact simply because it is new and unfamiliar. Remember, Truth can only help and heal. *It is falsehood that hurts.* See this by personal experiment. For example, notice how much better you feel when admitting and correcting a mistake. Know why you feel better? Because you are that much closer to your spiritual home.

17. God helps pretenders who want to stop pretending. This is a world of pretense. You have noticed this. People pretend they are not scared, pretend they are not hurt, pretend they are not nervous. Wearing masks of strength and confidence to impress people, they cry inside. Pretense is harmful and unnecessary. It fills space that should be filled with Reality. Wherever you see your own pretense, drop it. Its pain will vanish.

18. Constantly remember and practice S.O.S. Imagine a ship turning its spotlight down onto a stormy sea. The light reveals the storm but is not part of it. The storm cannot touch or harm the light, for their natures are different.

When life gets stormy, practice S.O.S., which means Spotlight on Storm. Remain in the calm light of your real self. *That by itself is help from God.* You will see your problems and tensions fall away all by themselves, like leaves falling from a tree.

19. Reality is ready to give you your rights. Everyone races around screaming for his rights, wrecking himself and the world. God gives you the right: a. To be a sane and decent human being. b. To not be hurt by anything in life. c. To exchange anxiety for peace. d. To know who you really are. e. To possess Eternal Life. Anyone can have these rights—anyone who ceases to imitate a lunatic society which demands its right to destroy itself.

20. Know that an idea about God is not God. People have thousands of strange ideas about God based on personal desires and fears. People are not in contact with God at all, but pray only to their own *idea* about God. No mere idea about something is the object itself. A thought about an apple is not an actual apple. God

18

exists in a Reality above all human thought. To reach God's help, rise above your own human thoughts. Do this by seeing their limitations.

21. *Remember who your true friends are.* A spy crept into enemy country with memorized names of friends who would help him. But when bumping his head in an accident he forgot the names. He was terrified at being alone in enemy country. But his homeland sent him the names again, and he was safe. Don't fear this world. Just ask God to help you remember your true and only friends, which are spiritual truths. Rely on them.

22. *Don't take nervousness as necessary.* Obey this simple spiritual instruction and your days will be inspired. People don't see how badly they treat themselves. Test it for yourself. Do you consider nervousness to be unpleasant, useless, harmful? Of course. Then why tolerate it? Only because you don't as yet know the alternative of poise and self-command. These virtues arrive by *refusing to take nervousness* *as necessary*. Mentally refuse at first, after which your whole spirit will refuse.

23. Realize that understanding is everything.
Some troubled people sought help from a Wise Man. He instructed, "Never do anything with a problem except to try to understand it. Don't try to win over anyone, don't angrily defend yourself, don't fear the situation. You *can* understand, so pour all your energies into this aim. An understood problem is *no* problem." Understanding is the highest form of action you can perform. It makes you comfortable.

24. Understand that Truth alone will never betray you. Ever been tricked and hurt by evil people? Maybe you can still hear them laughing at how they fooled you. You were betrayed because you trusted human weakness instead of spiritual strength. That is like trusting a flock of vicious vultures to behave like innocent doves. *Insight into human cruelty is the same as help from God.* Never forget this. Watch how it helps. It places you in command of yourself, after which you command conditions.

25. *You need not feel sad or defeated.* A teacher was walking the seashore with his students when he said, "See the waves flood over the rocks. Don't let harmful emotions flood over you." You can stop being overwhelmed by unhappy feelings *if you see them coming soon enough.* Be aware as sadness or defeat starts to rise and try to take you over. Your very awareness of it happening works like magic to stop it from happening. Awareness is spiritual power.

26. *Walk toward a new and different world.* A new world exists for you just as surely as Venus exists. It is inner, truly spiritual, ruled by Reality. It awaits your discovery. March toward this higher life right now by seeing what it is *not.* It is not like this world. It has no confusion, no fear of loss, no loneliness, no self-destructive acts. Change yourself and it is your world! Be eager to make this inner change. Years from now you will see it as the wisest decision of your life.

27. *Get out of the tension trap.* You can

21

unlearn tension with these two steps: a. Be aware of physical tension. b. Deliberately relax from it. Run your attention over yourself to detect stressful states. Examples: tense hands, anxious voice, tight jaw, nervous face. Now, consciously relax. Let go of yourself. This sends an invitation to mind and emotions: "Please be calm like me." They will obey! Now you are receptive to Higher Truth!

28. Realize that ordinary thoughts cannot contact God. This explains why past attempts to reach higher help have failed. Usual thought is filled with egotism, which blocks contact. Contact comes with a sincere and persistent *request for contact.* It is like a man in a national park who wants to cross to the other side of a wide river, but sees no bridge. He asks a park ranger, who shows him the bridge. Have an attitude that requests help. You will be shown the bridge to a brighter land.

29. You are not chained to an unhappy past. Truth has no interest in anyone's past mistakes or shames. It simply wants you to realize that today is not yesterday. *You are not tied to a foolish self of yesterday. You are only wrongly tied to an unhappy memory of an experience of yesterday.* Study these two sentences for several weeks. Did weeds grow in the meadow last year? New seeds will fill the meadow with springtime flowers.

30. *Egotism is an enemy who pretends to be a friend.* Egotism is the cause of every human problem on earth. Think of some people who you know are the slaves of their egotism. See how their misery is caused by their self-conceit? Egotism is the cruel thief of true life. Remember, *it always pretends to be on your side,* but it is cunningly and fiercely against all that is good for you. The very recognition of this fact attracts new help from God. Dissolve this enemy of pleasurable days.

31. *Do not settle for a false feeling of life.* A false feeling of life arises from harmful emotions such as anger, envy, fear, depression. It is a thrill without insight. Being fiery and exciting, they try to make you think that they are giving you life. The fact is, they give you only what they are—dark defeat *masquerading* as life. Watch how they try to trick you, then settle only for true life. Now you will find pleasure in your own company.

32. Obey your deep yearning to return home. Have you ever quarreled with and parted from someone you cared for? Remember the dozens of agonizing emotions that flowed thru you? You yearned to return to that person, but wounded pride prevented it. You felt that *everything* would be all right if only you and he were together again. Well, ignore your pride and obey your deep wish to return to Reality. Your sensing is right. Everything *will* be all right.

33. People don't see that they don't see. An elephant was led in front of a man who feared elephants. When told to look at it he asked, "What elephant?" We must first see our weakness. Then we can see our strength. But people refuse to see anything that would expose their self-images of being pleasant or competent. They can't see that true pleasantness and competence exist above mere self-pictures. So to be free, *see*.

34.   *Never give value to suffering.* Millions do, which is why their pains persist. Agony is a false life which they foolishly value over true and peaceful life. For example, people love to fight. The love of pain separates you from God, for God has nothing to do with anguish. Never listen to suffering when it tells you it is good and necessary. It is deceiving you. Listen to Truth. This is an example of a strong spiritual fact which most people don't want to hear. Want out? Hear it.

35.   *Maintain healthy views of yourself.* Wholesome self-views send out requests to God, which are honored. So to send out good requests, see yourself as someone who: a. Can no longer believe in society's cruel lies. b. Needs help from a higher source than human intellects. c. Is willing to give up the harmful thrills of ego-victories over others. d. Dares to see what exists beyond present ways. e. Can take a simple truth and let it turn into a new strength.

36. You can avoid painful traps. A man reflected, "My unhappiness is caused by getting what I want, for my gains soon turn to pains. To be happy I need only to not want something before I get it!" Have you ever obtained a desired person or activity only to later regret it? That proves there was no real value in your goal—only imaginary value. Spiritual light will show you the difference between compulsive wants and natural needs. Then you will never again lead yourself into a painful trap.

37. Don't credit human beings with power. Don't be impressed by leaders of society. Don't be in awe of anyone. No one created himself. A man walks across the room with energy supplied by God, not by himself. This is why you need not fear anyone or anything, including your own weakness. You are not dependent upon yourself for strength and wisdom. See this! It connects you permanently with Truth, the only source of true power.

38. *Go thru the temporary discomfort of being wrong*. Find it hard to admit you are wrong about your life?   Well, listen to this. Nothing will do more to make you overflow with strength and success.   Remember, it is not *you* who is wrong, but your old and false nature that is exposed as wrong. A spiritual teacher gave insight to his students when he asked them, "Why defend the wrongness that torments you?" Be wrong, for after that you will be both right and strong!

39. *Replace frantic action with quiet seeing*. Society is like a maniac wildly driving a truck with his eyes closed. Look at all the human wrecks! Look at all the sorrow! Let this re-mind you to slow down your life to where you can ask, "Where am I going and why?" Never mind the reckless drivers who want only fast thrills and self-glory. You were called to make a marvelous discovery. Quietly see that you have a True Treasure to find.

40. *Understand that you presently cannot make right decisions*. All you can do is to fall into one of several wrong moves. Face this fact. Then detect tricky ideas that present themselves as solutions—and refuse them. A feeling of peaceful self-release will flow thru you. This happens because you no longer try to carry burdens that you cannot carry. Now decisions no longer come *from* you, but *to* you. They come from a high spiritual level. Power and help from this lofty level is inexhaustible.

41. *You need not try to prove anything to anyone.* Notice how people anxiously try to prove they are right or wise or loving. This nervous and needless effort separates them from Truth's quiet kingdom. Simply don't try to prove that you are this or that kind of person. *You need not be someone who must try to prove he is someone!* Take as long as is necessary to understand this. It guarantees an easy life, which is Truth's reward to you.

42. *Let the answers to life come to you.* An explorer seeking a long-lost city in the jungle made camp for the night. Someone asked him about the best direction for tomorrow's march.

He replied, "I'm waiting to hear from head-quarters." Employ this wisdom. *If you refuse long enough to say what is best for you in life the true answer will come from Higher Head-quarters.* Wish to be free of painful thoughts? You can be free. Want a true and lasting feeling of security? It will come.

43. *You can know why life happens as it does.* People cry out, "I don't know what's happening to me or why!" Life to them is like a man tumbled about by a whirlwind, helpless and terrified. Understand spiritual laws and it won't happen to you anymore. For example, a man is betrayed by power-hungry friends because he was himself power-greedy. You see wrongness in others by first seeing it in yourself. This is perfect protection.

44. *Move to a new internal location.* A wealthy man owned a luxurious home on top of a hill. His neighbors envied him, but he had a sad secret. He knew his home was built on soft ground and could sag and break at any moment. Finally, sensibly, he moved to a new home. His nervousness vanished. Truth invites you to learn how to move to a new and safe place inside yourself. Accept the invitation. You can start by seeing how tired you are of your present internal location.

45. *Enrich your mind and enrich your life.* Notice how your mind connects with everything in your day. You *think* about money, *think* about food, *think* about sex. Your mind is like an electrical powerhouse that sends energy into your actions. Let God supply you with a higher quality of thought-energy, which brightens everything. Your part is to *suspect that you are being tricked by harmful thoughts.* That breaks their power forever.

46. *You need not strain after answers to life.* Instead of trying to create your own answers to problems, let Truth reveal them. See the difference in the two words *create* and *reveal*. When you try to create answers you get the same false solutions from the same level of human confusion, which is why nothing really changes. Stop strained effort. See what it means to be in the right place inwardly. Be like the hungry man who stood below a fruit orchard and let the apples roll down to him!

47. *Listen to something besides your present nature.* Your present self has attracted all your troubles, so refuse to obey it anymore. Listen to a higher voice. Be like the man who wanted to hear a nightingale sing, so he climbed the mountain where it lived. Climb the spiritual mountain. Practice at listening to voices that tell you it is wrong to do certain acts. Listen and obey them. You will contact Truth, the perfect guide thru life.

48. *Never protect yourself against failure.* People fight fiercely to prevent what they call personal failure. Having strong ambitions, they hate and hurt others whom they blame for their defeat. If you will go far enough in not shielding your ego-nature from failure you will see a miracle of inner freedom. You will see there was no one to fail and therefore no failure at all. This places you above human success and failure and peacefully with True Success. Act fully on this. What a relief!

49. *See that religion is not the same as spirituality.* Religion is outside, spirituality is inside. Religion does not require you to take an honest look at how you behave, but spirituality does. People rarely see the difference, but God does. Using religious words does not make a man spiritual any more than talking about gold makes him valuable. Religion needs other people, but you can be spiritual all alone. Be spiritual by placing Truth above all else. God's help follows.

50. *Let absolutely nothing prevent your return home.* A young prince wasted his life in useless wandering. He finally returned to the castle and asked to be let in, but the gate remained closed. Each day for a whole year he approached the gate and tried to get in, but failed. But on the first day of the second year the gate opened. His persistence showed his father that he really wanted to change his life. Persist in your wish for the royal life. The gate will open before you!

Meet
Vernon Howard

VERNON HOWARD is a unique teacher who has broken through to another world. He sees through the illusion of suffering and fear and loneliness.

His books are widely used by doctors, psychologists, clergymen, educators, etc. He shows you exactly how to end all problems. Read his inspiring books and see for yourself!

VERNON HOWARD lives and teaches in Boulder City, Nevada.

Discover the Wonderful World of
VERNON HOWARD

POWERFUL BOOKS
   Treasury of Positive Answers
   Psycho-Pictography
   The Power of Your Supermind
   The Mystic Masters Speak
   Inspire Yourself
   The Mystic Path to Cosmic Power
   There is a Way Out
   1500 Ways to Escape the
      Human Jungle
   Esoteric Mind Power

ENRICHING BOOKLETS
   50 Ways to See Thru People
   Conquer Anxiety and Frustration
   Your Power to Say No
   Sex and Sweethearts
   50 Ways to Get Help from God
   Women: 50 Ways to See Thru Men

Booklets - continued
Be Safe in a Dangerous World
Conquer Harmful Anger 100 Ways
Live Above This Crazy World

INSPIRING CASSETTE TAPES
The Help You Really Want to Find
Never Again Be Blamed and Hurt
Secrets the Whole World Should Hear
Your Treasure of Higher Pleasure
Conquer Stress While Sleeping
The Law of Spiritual Development

Ask your local bookseller for powerful VERNON HOWARD books, booklets and cassette tapes—or write today for a free complete list and order form:

NEW LIFE
Box 684, Boulder City, Nevada 89005

NEW LIFE
Box 2000, Ojai, California 93023
Have something nice to look forward to!

Invitation

Please send us the names and addresses of friends who may be interested in these helpful teachings. We will send them our free literature.

Also, for your own information on books, tapes and classes write: